C0-GLU-520

Wild About Watercolor

Henry County Libraries
Fortson Public Library
14 Old Griffin Rd.
Hampton, GA 30228

HENRY COUNTY LIBRARY SYSTEM
HAMPTON, LOCUST GROVE, McDONOUGH, STOCKBRIDGE

Written by
Wes Clark

Walter Foster

Illustrated by
Diana Fisher

© 1999, Walter Foster Publishing, Inc. All rights reserved.
Walter Foster Publishing, Inc., 23062 La Cadena Drive, Laguna Hills, CA 92653
This book has been published to aid the aspiring artist.
Reproduction of the work for study or finished art is permissible.
Any art drawn or photomechanically reproduced from this publication for commercial purposes
is forbidden without written consent from the publisher, Walter Foster Publishing, Inc.
Printed in Hong Kong.

Dive In and Begin!

Welcome to the world of water and paint!
It's fun and it's easy—you'll have no complaint.
The first thing to do is to gather your tools,
and then we'll start out with a few simple rules.

Let's see, you'll want paper (the watercolor kind),
your palette of paints, whatever tape you can find.
And of course you'll be needing a big cup of water,
a sponge, and some tissue to use as a blotter.

Add a toothbrush, a marker, and even a crayon,
plus scissors, some salt, and a surface to play on.
But have we forgotten one thing in the rush?
Oh, that's right (how silly!)—you **will** need a brush!

Hey, What's the Brush?

ne brush is enough, but more would be better.
ome will stay dry, and some will get wetter.
wide one, a fine one, an average one too—
variety gives you more things you can do.

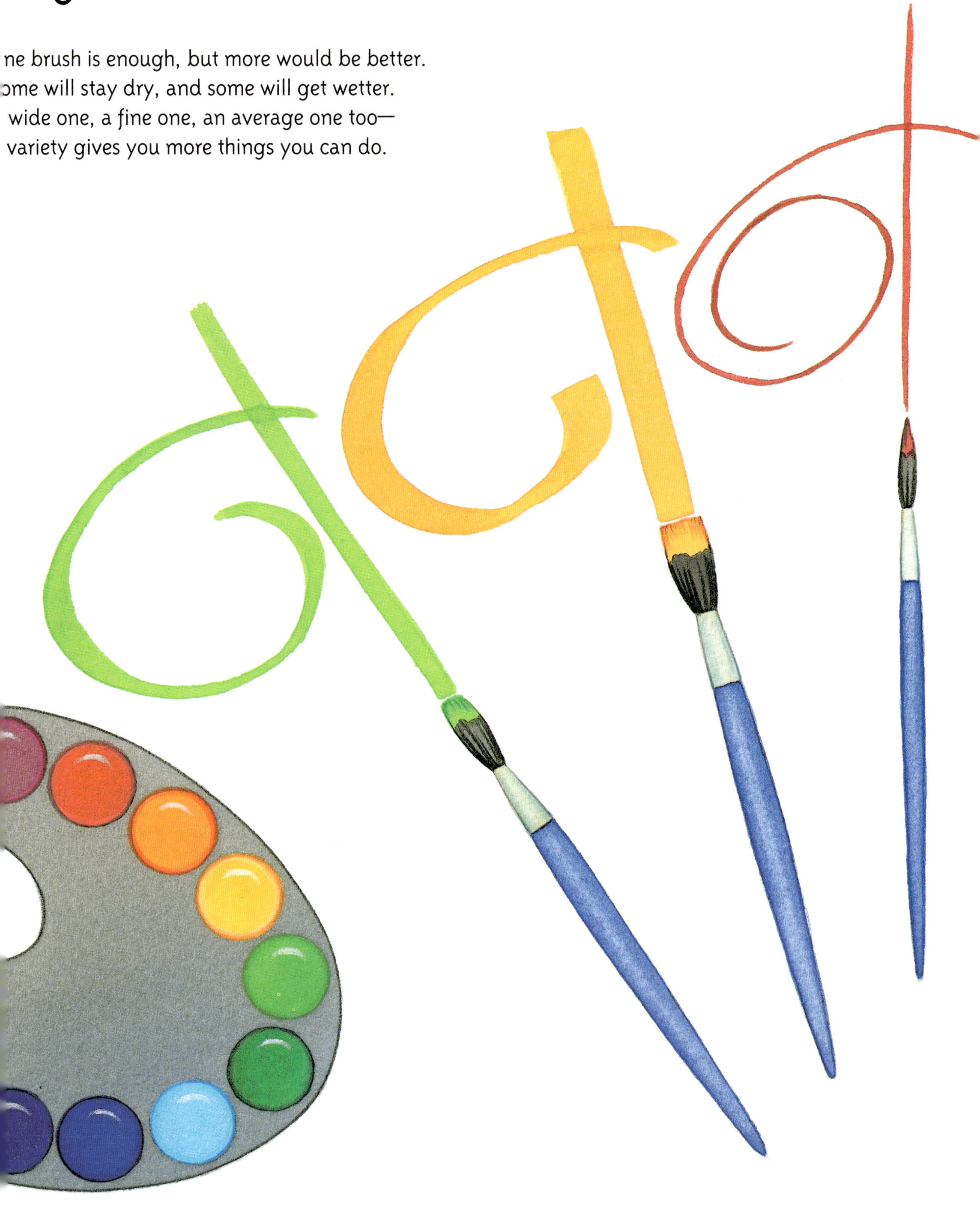

Fixin' on the Mixin'!

Mixing the colors is sort of a science.
You match up a pair, and they form an alliance.
The color wheel shows you what colors to mix
to make three new colors—so then you'll have six!

You needn't be Einstein to learn this equation:
Yellow plus blue equals green—new creation!
And that's just for starters; there're more you can try
to make flowers or grass or a big dragonfly.

Brush Strokes for Creative Folks!

Different shaped brushes make different sized lines,
and how you apply them can change the designs.
How hard you press down can determine a lot.
Press hard, the line's fat; press softly, it's not.

Make long simple strokes for the rainbow's bright stripes,
and paint the duck's feathers in smooth yellow swipes.
Use short strokes to make rays that show the sun shining,
and carefully outline the cloud's bright blue lining.

How can you finish this rainy day scene?
It's really quite easy—here, see what we mean?
Press down with your brush, and then lift it away.
It may take some practice, but you'll learn the way!

Shape It with Tape!

Here's a wonderful way to make lines that are straight
or create some white space—if it isn't too late!
Just roll out some tape, and press it down first.
The sticky kind's best—videotape is the worst!

To paint a cool kite just as Freddy's done here,
make shapes with some tape—either masking or clear.
Then paint the inside with your favorite hue;
pull the tape up—see what "sticking to it" can do!

Pitter Patter, Here Comes the Splatte

Here's another technique that you surely will love.
Just splatter on color with specks from above!
Get a toothbrush you're through with and won't use again;
spread newspapers out—you're not ready 'til then.

Now paint a whole scene, and as soon as you're through,
let's see what that old worn-out toothbrush can do!
First get it wet and put paint on its bristles;
run your finger across, making colorful missiles!

Lunge for That Sponge!

Lots of everyday things can become painting tools.
You don't have to use brushes; there aren't any rules!
Try painting with sponges you've torn into chunks,
or use your own scissors to cut out some hunks.

Next soak up some water; then squeeze it back out.
A sponge that's too wet won't work well, there's no doubt.
Now dab it in paint; you can choose any color.
Make some things look brighter and others look duller.

You Ought to Blot!

Here's a way to remove spots of color while wet;
but "blotting" works only with paint that's not set.
Paper towels and tissues can both soak up water;
pick one or the other to use as a blotter.

Hurry now—blot it before it gets dry!
Scrunch up your towel, and give it a try.
Would you like to add clouds to a sky of light blue?
Now think of what other neat things you can do!

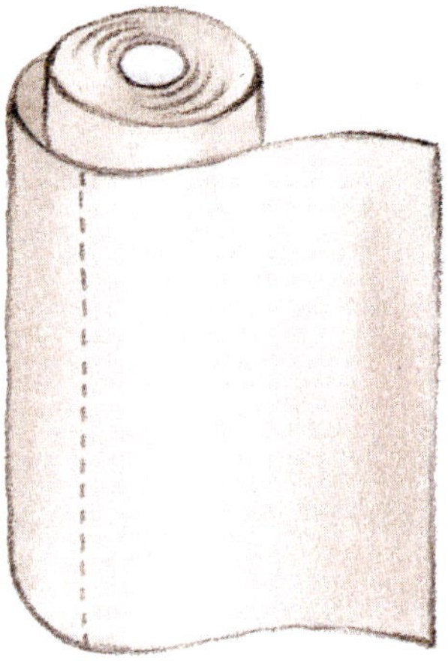

Oh Gosh, It's Time for a Wash!

We're not talkin' 'bout bathtime, if that's what you think.
But you **will** need some water, so head for the sink.
First get your brush wet, and then get it wetter.
Remember: for washes, the wetter, the better!

Next, dab up some paint, but don't use too much,
and sweep back and forth with an artistic touch.
Your brush should glide smoothly, but don't let it slosh;
just stroke left to right and voilà—it's a wash!

Gradation Sensation!

It's fun to make colors that blend in a stream,
from darker to lighter without any seam.
We call this **gradation,** a simple technique,
and you'll be an expert in less than a week!

Try painting a lavender wash for a starter.
It gradually gets paler by adding more water.
Go over the light part with blue, so they blend.
Then "gradate" straight down to pure blue at the end.

Wet on Wet? You Bet!

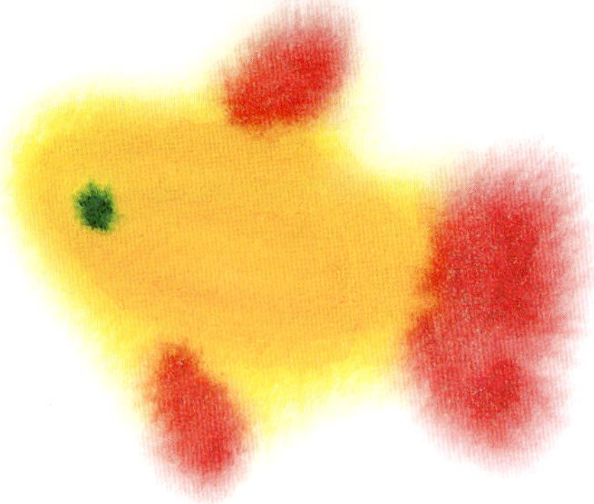

It's all great so far, but you wonder if whether
there isn't some way to make the paint "feather."
Just start out by making the **whole** paper wet.
It won't be a problem; there's no need to fret!

Now brush on some color to fill up the page,
but don't let it dry; leave it damp at this stage.
While it's still wet, add a blue and green fish,
then seaweed and coral—whatever you wish!

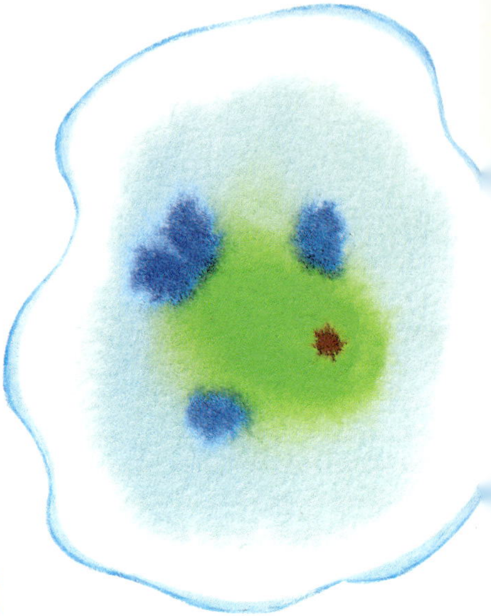

Make It Lush with Drybrush!

Now, water's important, so don't get us wrong,
but there's only one way to get colors this strong.
Use very little water for hues that are bright,
and load up on color—that's doing it right!

Wipe your brush on a towel to take off some paint;
so your strokes will have places where color is faint.
This drybrush technique can be used anywhere;
it adds a rought coat to this furry brown bear.

HONEY

It's All Right to Leave White!

To use watercolor, you needn't have white.
Instead just leave part of your paper in sight.
For a fun way to do this, you cut out a stencil;
then outline the shape with a pen or a pencil.

To make it look fancy, just fill in the shape
with stripes, dots, or solids—don't let them escape!
Inside all the lines is where color is placed;
if paint gets outside them, it can't be erased!

Pass the Salt, Please!

We know salt adds flavor to food; this is true.
But did you know it can "spice up" paintings too?
Ask your parents if you can please use the salt shaker.
(They may wonder if you are an artist or baker!)

While the color is wet, give the shaker a sprinkle,
Salt pushes paint out with an interesting wrinkle.
Then blow the salt off when your painting is dry.
The effect that it leaves looks like stars in the sky!

An Outline Is Fine!

Another great way to make paintings look neat,
is to start with an outline—it's not a tough feat.
It's a special technique many great artists use,
and you can learn how if you follow their cues.

You'll need special pens—get the kind that won't smudge.
"Indelible" or "permanent" ink will not budge.
Use the pen to make drawings with curved or straight lines;
then paint in the shapes to make colored designs.

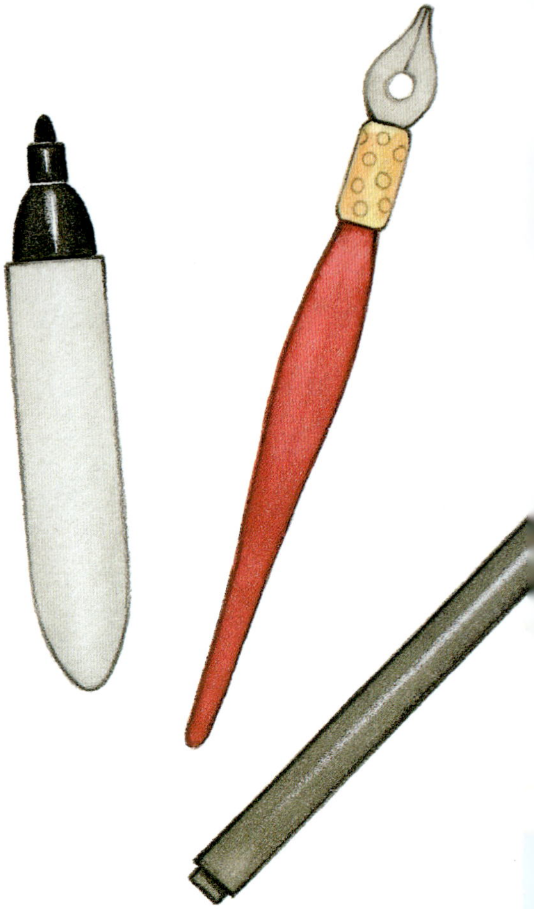

YOU'RE RIGHT ON TRACK! KEEP PRACTICING!

You Can't Resist This!

Crayons and paint can add new variations
when they are combined in artistic creations.
First choose what to paint—maybe objects or shapes,
like checkerboard patterns or fruit (even grapes).

Color lightly with crayon; don't make it too thick,
or there won't be a place for the wet paint to stick.
The textures you get when you use this technique
will make any painting you do look unique!

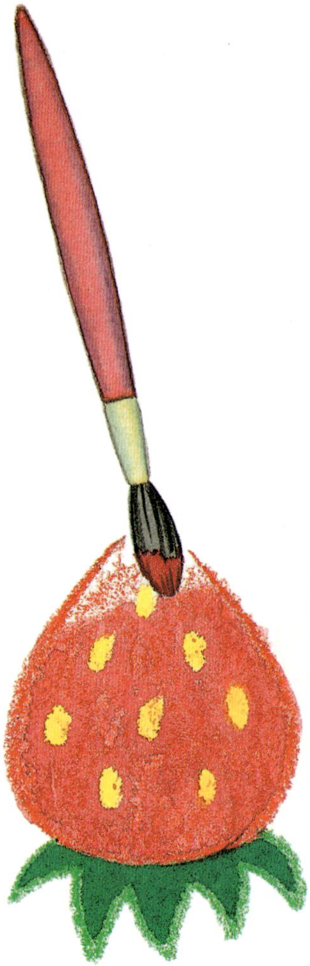

Picture This!

Now that you're done, here's a project to do:
Make a frame for those photos that mean most to you.
Get your scissors, your tape, and your pencil and brush.
(Be careful with scissors; there's no need to rush!)

Paint the front of the paper; use all that you've learned.
When it's dry, it can be touched or picked up and turned.
Draw shapes on the back, and then cut them all out.
Now tape in those photos we just talked about.

There, now you have made one—your own picture frame!
This could be your first step to glory and fame!
Keep practicing painting, and have lots of fun.
With **Paint Pandemonium,** the fun's never done!

Henry County Libraries
Fortson Public Library
14 Old Griffin Rd.
Hampton, GA 30228